Parents' Guide To the Basics Manual

Published by New Generation Publishing in 2020

Paperback ISBN: 978-1-80031-873-1

www.newgeneration-publishing.com

New Generation Publishing

Parents' Guide to the Basics Manual

by

K.M. MacPhee

MA, EdB, PhD

Numbers 1 to 10

It is essential that children completely understand the concept of the numbers 1 to 10, before going on to 11 and above.

It is advised to practise the numerals and their corresponding words, on a regular basis until understanding and complete familiarity are reached.

Number lines, stories, pictures and rhymes are a good way of reinforcing familiarity with numbers.

You can make up a story about, eg Sally the Kitten, introduce the numbers, talk about them with your child, and get the child to draw a picture of the story. Obviously the story can be about any subject you like, the more familiar the better.

The following is an example of the sort of story based on the numbers 1 to 10.

Here is

the story

of 10

1 one

Here is Sally Kitten.
She has 1 mummy cat
and 1 daddy cat.

2 two

1 2
One two

That makes 2 cats .
They each have 2 eyes and 2 ears .

3 Three

1 2 3
One two three

Sally has 2 brothers, Fluff and Tigger.
Sally, Fluff and Tigger make 3 kittens.
3 kittens have 3 tails and
3 noses.

4 Four

1 2 3 4
One two three four

Sally, Fluff and Tigger
have a friend called Daisy.
Now there are 4 kittens.
Each kitten has 4 paws.
Daisy has 4 spots on her tail.

Can you see 4 different things in your room, like chairs, books, pictures, toys?

Count them :-

1 2 3 4

One, two, three, four

5 Five

Here is Daisy's sister, Dora. 4 kittens and 1 kitten make 5 kittens. Sally counts them all :- Fluff, Tigger, Daisy, Dora and me.

That is 1 2 3 4 5

One, two, three, four five, she says.

6 Six

It's time to go to school.
The 5 kittens see 6 cars in the street.

1 2 3 4 5 6
One, two, three, four, five, six

3 are red and 3 are blue. That makes 6.
4 are small and 2 are big.
That makes 6
3 and 3 are 6,
and 4 and 2 are 6,
and 5 and 1 are six.

7 seven

Sally meets her friends Peter Piglet and Sammy Squirrel. The 7 little animals all play together.

1 2 3 4 5 6 7
One, two, three, four, five, six, seven

There are 5 kittens, 1 piglet and 1 squirrel. That makes 7 animals.
5 are playing football and 2 are talking.

8 eight

There are 8 desks in the classroom.

1 2 3 4 5 6 7 8
One, two, three, four, five, six, seven, eight

5 desks are in one row.
3 desks are in the other. That makes 8.
Mr Rabbit, the teacher, is
counting everyone:
Sally, Fluff, Tigger, Daisy and Dora in this row. That's 5.
Peter and Sammy are in the other row. That's 2.
7 full desks and 1 empty desk. That's 8 desks.

9 nine

Mr Rabbit has 9 picture books.

1 2 3 4 5 6 7 8 9
One, two, three, four, five, six,
seven, eight, nine

He gives 1 to everyone in the class:
1 to Sally, 1 to Fluff, 1 to Tigger,
1 to Daisy, 1 to Dora, 1 to Peter and 1 to Sammy. That makes 7.
Oh, there are 2 left over.
7 and 2 makes 9.
There are 5 red books, 2 blue books and 2 green books.
5 and 2 and 2 make 9.

10 ten

Here comes Mr Rabbit with 10 balls for everyone to play with.

1 2 3 4 5 6 7 8 9 10
One, two, three, four, five, six, seven, eight, nine, ten

The 1st one is for Sally
The 2nd one is for Fluff
The 3rd one is for Tigger
The 4th one is for Daisy
The 5th one is for Dora
The 6th one is for Peter
The 7th one is for Sammy
The 8th one is left over
So is the 9th one
And so is the 10th one.

Number line of 10

10
9
8
7
6
5
4
3
2
1
0

Here are 2 little rhymes about 10

One, two buckle my shoe

1, 2 buckle my shoe
3, 4 shut the door
5, 6 pick up sticks
7, 8 shut the gate

9,10 a big fat hen!

Ten Green Bottles

10 green bottles sitting on the wall
10 green bottles sitting on the wall
And if 1 green bottle should accidentally fall
There'll be 9 green bottles sitting on the wall.

9 green bottles sitting on the wall
9 green bottles sitting on the wall
And if 1 green bottle should accidentally fall
There'll be 8 green bottles sitting on the wall.

Continue like this down to 0/ no green bottles.
Point out that the number lower than 1 on the number line is 0.

Numbers from 10 to 20

Introduce the words "add" and "plus", and the symbol + Show the number line from 10 to 20 :

20
19
18
17
16
15
14
13
12
11
10

11 is ten plus 1, or 10 + 1
12 is ten plus 2, or 10 + 2 and so on up to 20
Make up stories about the numbers, eg continuing on the cat theme:

Sally Kitten grew 14 carrots in her garden.
Brer Rabbit sneaked in when she wasn't looking. He ate 5. Then Toby Rabbit sneaked in and ate 5.
Andy Rabbit was annoyed because the others had left only 4 for him, so the 14th carrot was the last one.
Sally Kitten was annoyed because she didn't have any carrots left at all.

20 twenty

Point out that 20 is 10+10 and reinforce with a story, eg

Noah is in a hurry to get all the animals on to his ark. He has to put them on, 2 by 2, in pairs:
2 cows
2 sheep
2 goats
2 camels
2 lions
2 tigers
2 giraffes
2 elephants
2 monkeys
And only 1 crocodile

Noah wasn't happy.
"There are only 19 animals", he said.
"I must have 20 at least"

I need another crocodile, because 19 plus 1 makes 20. The animals weren't happy either.

They didn't want another crocodile.

They didn't even want 1 crocodile!

Continue introducing **ordinals** :
12th twelfth
16th sixteenth
20th twentieth, and so on.

Begin to associate the numbers 1-9 with the word **"units"**, eg 3 units, 7 units, etc
Show that 9 is the highest unit, and that 10 is actually 1 **"ten"** and 0 units.
11 is 1 ten and 1 unit
12 is 1 ten and 2 units
Continue up to 20, which is 2 tens and 0 units, 21 is 2 tens and 1 unit.
Continue up to 30, which is 3 tens and 0 units, and so on up to 100.
Introduce the word **"hundred"**.
And show that 100 is 1 hundred, 0 tens and 0 units,
101 is 1 hundred, 0 tens and 1 unit, and so on up to a thousand.

Follow the same pattern with the thousands .

30 thirty

The school bus collects 30 children going to school.
30 is 20 + 10

Show the number line :

30
29
28
27
26
25
24
23
22
21
20

When the bus stops at school 30 children get off.
The last one off is the 30th.

40 forty

40 is 30 + 10

Show the number line

40
39
38
37
36
35
34
33
32
31
30

Forty people are going to work on a train. The last one off is the 40th.

49
48
47
46
45
44
43
42
41
40
39
38
37
36
35
34
33
32
31
30
29
28
27
26
25
24
23
22
21
20
19
18
17
16
15
14
13
12
11
10
9
8
7
6
5
4
3
2
1
0

Continue with number lines going up in tens to 100, then show the number line 1-100, so that the child can see the continuity from 1 to 100:

100
99
98
97
96
95
94
93
92
91
90
89
88
87
86
85
84
83
82
81
80
79
78
77
76
75
74
73
72
71
70
69
68
67
66
65
64
63
62
61
60
59
58
57
56
55
54
53
52
51
50

Introduce a number line from 0 to 100 going up in jumps of 10:

100
90
80
70
60
50
40
30
20
10
0

Point out that the units numbers stay at 0 while the tens numbers go up 1, 2, 3, etc, as usual.

Introduce the number line from 100 to 1000 in jumps of 100

1000

900

800

700

600

500

400

300

200

100

Point out that the units and tens numbers stay at 0 while the hundreds go up 1,2,3,etc, as usual .

By these means the child will come to recognise the importance of **Place Value** :-

Units must stay with units, tens with tens, hundreds with hundreds, and so on.

This is essential before starting the maths part of the Basics Manual.
Reinforce all these steps by frequent use and repetition until everything is well established and understood.
It is well worthwhile spending time at this stage before embarking on more formal work.

Addition

Revise the symbol +, and the words "add" and "plus", eg

2 + 6, or 2 plus 6, means add 6 units to 2 units, and use a number line to show that you go **up** the line from 2 to 8 units. Similarly, show that 8 + 6, or 8 plus 6, takes you up the number line to 14, ie 1 ten and 4 units.
Use the number lines until the child has enough confidence to add without them.

Subtraction

Introduce the word "subtraction" meaning "taking away", the word "minus", and the symbol -
Simple subtraction is easy when the child can physically take something away, eg
5 buttons away from 8 buttons leaves 3 buttons, etc.
Practise concrete examples like this before going on to abstract examples, then use the number line to show that you go **down** the line when taking away (and **up** the line when adding).
Use the number line until counting can be done mentally.
With larger numbers, eg 25 - 13, or 25 minus 13, it should still be easy for the child to understand that to take away 3 units from 5 units leaves 2 units, and to take 1 ten away from 2 tens leaves 1 ten.
This can probably be more clearly seen when written formally:

$$\begin{array}{r} 25 \\ -\underline{13} \\ \underline{12} \end{array}$$

With this sum,

$$\begin{array}{r} 25 \\ -\underline{17} \\ \underline{8} \end{array}$$

there are 2 methods available:

a) equal additions

ie you can't take 7 units away if you have only 5 units, so add 1 ten to the 5 units, giving you 15 units.
You can now take the 7 units away from 15 units, giving 8 units. But because you have added 1 ten to the units, now you must add 1 ten to the tens ie, 1 ten becomes 2 tens. Take 2 tens away from 2 tens, and you are left with 0.

b) decomposition of number

This is a slower method than equal additions, but it is more logical.

Again, you can't take 7 units away if you have only 5 units, so take one of the tens and break it down into 10 units, leaving you with only 1 ten on the top line.
Add the 10 units to the 5 units, giving you 15 units.
You can now take away 7 units from 15 units, giving you 8 units. Now take away 1 ten from the 1 ten left on the top line. That gives you 0 tens.

Use the method which suits the child best.

Multiplication

Introduce the symbol x and the word "times", also the symbol = and the words "equal to".

Show how multiplication makes numbers get bigger, eg
4 + 4 = 8,
or 2 lots of 4 = 8
or 2 x 4 = 8:
and 3 + 3 + 3 + 3 = 12
or 4 lots of 3 = 12
or 4 x 3 = 12

Point out that it is easier and quicker when you learn the multiplication tables off by heart.

With larger numbers remind the child that it is essential to keep everything in its correct columns of units, tens, hundreds, etc., ie **Place Value**

Division

Introduce the symbol ÷, and the word "divide".
Explain that it means sharing, and that dividing numbers makes them get smaller, eg 15 ÷ 3 = 5, or
15 sweets shared equally among 3 boys will mean that each boy gets 5 sweets.
With larger numbers remind the child again that it is essential to keep everything in its correct columns of units, tens, hundreds, etc.

Going below 0

It is useful, at this stage, to show that numbers can go down below 0. This will be obvious on another number line , which can be as long or short as you wish it to be, eg :

14
13
12
11
10
9
8
7
6
5
4
3
2
1
0
-1
-2
-3
-4
-5
-6
-7
-8, etc

Show that 6 - 8 = - 2, by going **down** the number line, below 0. Similarly - 7 + 12 = 5, by going **up** the number line, above 0.
Practise this, using the number line until the child has enough confidence to work out these calculations without having to look at the number line.
This ability will be very useful when learning the beginnings of algebra, etc.

www.ingramcontent.com/pod-product-compliance
Ingram Content Group UK Ltd.
Pitfield, Milton Keynes, MK11 3LW, UK
UKHW051206260726
13967UKWH00011B/3135